To Be A Woman

To Be A Woman

THE EXPERIENCE OF WOMANHOOD

IN WRITINGS SELECTED BY LOIS DANIEL

AND ILLUSTRATED BY MURIEL WOOD

HALLMARK EDITIONS

Contents

Reflections

'OUR INNER LIFE'

In this selection from her book The Creative Woman, *Dorothy Goldberg wife of former United States Supreme Court Justice Arthur Goldberg, suggests reserving "a little energy for the other life within us":*

The doings of the day become our roots, and mothers are all trees of many roots standing by the ever-rushing water of time. And then, this too has passed. Some are glad; some are sorry. The important thing is to save some energy— even a little—because all the doings do not have to get done at once. There is no botulism brewing in the extra moment or two it takes to return something to the refrigerator.

What I am saying is that, as we rush about, we must reserve a little energy for that other life within us, that urge to make, to do, to try to create.

If we have one child, then our inner life becomes our second child. If we already have two children, then the life within us must be our third child. Even four, five, six. Even if there are six children to be helped toward their own launchings, the inner life must be her seventh child. If that inner life is built around art, then that is the child, and it must be given all the attention, concern and money we would somehow find if it were a child in the flesh. What we would spend for the gynecologist, the obstetrician and the education of a real child, those are the costs due that mythical child, the inner interest and inner life that are your own.

'LIFE BEGINS TOMORROW'

In her book How To Be A Happy Woman, *author Ardis Whitman describes the unrealistic attitude women sometimes have about their childhoods. Here she dispells the notion that it was all gossamer :*

"I had the most wonderful dream last night," said a friend of mine wistfully. "I dreamed I was a child again. Everything was just as clear. I was sitting in the swing under the apple tree and I had my kitten in my lap and Mother was hanging clothes on the line. Somehow I knew it was a dream and I tried so hard not to let it go that when I woke up I was crying."

It's a dream that comes to all of us, waking or

sleeping; for there is another past as sure in its fascination as grandma's golden age and there is no woman, however sophisticated, who has not felt its tug at her heart. . . .

Those were the days, you think. There's no getting around it. Youth is the time when you really know what it is to be happy! Things just *were* and there was nothing to worry about—no income tax, no atom bombs, no budgets that wouldn't balance. Then too, you didn't feel badgered about time. Time stood still or moved for you with infinite slowness; and there was always something waiting for you tomorrow—something unimaginable and wonderful.

Best of all, the world was full of romance. When you were sixteen, all you had to do was step outside of an evening and there it was!

I suppose men dredge up old memories too. When we're just plain bone-tired and things have gotten too much for us, all of us are prone to believe that we've left behind the good time, the best time. But men don't make as much fuss about it as women do. Maybe they never really left it; or perhaps it's just that it's so easy to start a woman dreaming. All it takes is a dried flower in a scrapbook; a love letter scuffling around in the dust on the attic floor; the smell of lilacs on a June night; or the sound of bees in a hayfield on

a summer afternoon—and there you are, dripping tears and certain that all of happiness was somehow tied up with a boy whose face you've forgotten and whose thoughts you never knew.

So women are sentimental! "What's wrong with that?" you ask. What's the matter with dreaming away an April afternoon by an old trunk in an attic?

Nothing perhaps—if you can smile at the end and put all the trinkets back in place and think to yourself, "It *was* fun, while I had it—but it's so much less than I have now." The trouble is that millions of us don't believe that. According to the Gallup poll, the average American wishes to be a child again; and millions of women never get beyond the child's concept of what it means to be happy. It's bad enough that we use our memories as a place to run when things go wrong; but there's something we do that's a great deal worse. We use them as a criterion of happiness, counting as loss everything that isn't the way it was when we were children.

So maybe we ought to do a little debunking here and now. The simple truth is that memory is not nearly so trustworthy as we think. No, it's a compound of what life really was and what now we wish it could be.

The truth is we forget what it was like to be a

child. We forget about being told what to do and never having a chance to decide for ourselves. We forget how little we knew and how much we wanted to know. We forget how easily embarrassed we were, how sure that people were laughing at us. . . .

If the truth were told, these years were, for many people, what Ilka Chase calls "the badlands of life." Our sorrows and problems were worse for us when we were children because then we knew so little about how to solve them. Haven't you ever heard a frustrated and helpless youngster say, "Just wait till I'm big?" One of the best things about being very young is that you are so sure it will be fun to grow up!

No, there is something very wrong if these are the happiest hours of your life. "Show me a man or woman who is forever saying that all children are lucky merely by being children," says [Carl] Van Doren, "and I will show you a man or woman who is not doing so well as an adult."

Look back at childhood with love and affection but not with admiration. Chuckle delightedly; do not weep. Bring your wisdom to children; not vice versa. "Life begins tomorrow," says the Italian proverb. The secret is always to put much ahead of you; then you need not covet what you have left behind.

HARDSHIP PASSES ON

"Then Anna was born, so I had four babies to care for. But we got along very nice till the children got the scarlet fever, that was a hard year but it passed on like all the rest."

These two sentences constitute Grandma Moses' complete and unabridged account of one of her ninety-two years.

Its brevity, I believe, goes far to explain why Grandma . . . lived into her tenth decade. She is not inarticulate. She can describe in loving and minute detail, after sixty years, her wedding dress, a Thanksgiving dinner, a practical joke she and another girl played; but about a hard year she found nothing worth remembering except that "it passed on like all the rest."

Nobody can explain genius, so exactly what it is that makes Grandma Moses a magnificent painter no man can tell. But if you want to know why she . . . remained alert, vigorous, radiantly alive into her nineties, mull over the above bit of philosophy.

Beauty, love, laughter and delight are imperishable memories, but all that is important about hardship is that it passes on.

GERALD W. JOHNSON

'WHAT IS MY RESPONSIBILITY'

In this selection author Dorothy Hopper examines a woman's responsibilities in contrast to fulfillment of personal pleasure, asking herself the question, "What does life require of me?":

What a furtive hope is pleasure. For life does not deal with us so tenderly as to cater to our personal desires. Life deals us a set of cards, and then says, "Here, see what you can do with them." To take an unbalanced or mediocre hand and play it brilliantly—this is what makes the game exciting. Even when choice seems non-existent, life can be an act of declaration rather than the course of least resistance. One asks oneself over the morning dishes and in the dead of night, "What shall I do with my life?" If the answer is primarily a self-centered one, it is sure to be limiting and eventually unsatisfying.

If a woman matures as she ages, a time comes when she will put aside the wish, "Oh, what I long to be," and ask herself, "What does life require of me?" She ceases the yearning, "What would give me greatest pleasure," and demands of herself, "What is my responsibility?"

When she has decided what her responsibility shall be, she has also determined her goals, her purposes in life and her daily philosophy. It is

important to think of responsibility in the broadest possible terms: family, world, community and self. It is helpful to think through one's philosophy in a fairly specific way. I have set forth my own thoughts in this way: "My purpose in life is to make it possible for every living person (myself included) to develop his or her own potentialities in the greatest measure, and to live creatively according to his or her own possibilities." I work to achieve this in my personal family relationships, through my husband's work, through community service and in support of organizations and political candidates dedicated to this purpose on a national and international level.

THE REALISTS OF THE RACE

Here American author H. L. Mencken attributes a finely honed sense of reality to women, a sense of logic not possessed by men:
Women decide the larger questions of life correctly and quickly, not because they are lucky guessers, not because they are divinely inspired, not because they practice a magic inherited from savagery, but simply and solely because they have sense. They see at a glance what most men

could not see with searchlights and telescopes; they are at grips with the essentials of a problem before men have finished debating its mere externals. They are the supreme realists of the race. Apparently illogical, they are the possessors of a rare and subtle super-logic. Apparently whimsical, they hang to the truth with a tenacity which carries them through every phase of its incessant, jelly-like shifting of form.

IN DEFENSE OF BRAINS

Actress Nina Foch points out that women can reveal their intelligence without fear of men's disapproval or condemnation:

Heaven knows, women harbor some strange notions, but one of the strangest is the conviction that their brains are like icebergs—only one eighth should show above the surface. I have never understood why female intelligence should be concealed along with the family scandals, but time and again I've seen women pulling in their brains when a man appeared, afraid the poor thing might scratch his ego on the exposed edges.

Having brains and hiding them makes as much sense for a woman as owning a mink coat and keeping it permanently in cold storage. If she wears them with modesty and tact, not only will she be happier—but her men will, too.

'TO LOVE AND BE LOVED'

Author of many inspirational works, Faith Baldwin writes of the "capacity to love and to be loved" in this section from Living by Faith:

It has been said that we bring nothing into this world and take nothing with us when we depart. But that was written of material possessions. All of us bring with us the need to love and to be loved and take with us, in spirit, the knowledge of having loved and having been loved. As the infant grows and the formative years begin, this necessity for giving and receiving is conditioned by many things: environment, circumstances, the people around us, the discovery of personal prejudice, the emotional drives, and the opinions toward which they lead us. Often we find ourselves able to receive, yet not to give; or able to give, but feeling we have had little in return. Yet the basic needs remain. You see them in the baby barely conscious of the world about him . . . .

So in the new year I wish . . . always for the capacity to love and to be loved. I wish for the ability to remember the good things and forget

the rest, to create new memories and to be sustained by trust and hope and courage; and always to try to understand.

'THE SECRET OF HAPPINESS'

Couturiere Coco Chanel clothes the body and frees the mind. The witty Frenchwoman talks here about women and happiness:
Happiness is the secret of beauty. But who knows the secret of happiness? The wise woman keeps her cosmetics at hand.

Happiness is what you sometimes find when you pursue something else.

There are many more attempts to define happiness than unhappiness. It is because people know all too well what unhappiness is.

Some people pursue unhappiness because happiness is too mild a sensation.

Unhappiness is more dramatic—or, rather, melodramatic—and they see themselves at the center of the stage.

One should not seek happiness, but rather happy people.

To Love and Marry

In their book When You Marry, *authors Evelyn Duvall and Reuben Hill set the primary prerequisite for happy marriages, the ability to adjust:* When you come to marriage, what do you bring? A new wardrobe? A nest egg in the bank? Some furniture you've inherited? A dependent relative or two? A good job and the prospect of advancement? Whatever your tangible assets or liabilities are, there is something even more important: that is *you* as a personality, the way you act toward people and the attitudes which you bring to marriage.

The kind of marriage you make depends upon the kind of person you are. If you are a happy, well-adjusted person, the chances are your marriage will be a happy one. If you have made adjustments so far with more satisfaction than distress, you are likely to make your marriage and family adjustments satisfactorily. If you are discontented and bitter about your lot in life, you will have to change before you can expect to live happily ever after.

FAMILY ALBUM

On a photograph of my father
and mother just married

My parents, my children:
Who are you, standing there
In an old photograph—young married pair
I never saw before, yet see again?
You pose somewhat sedately side by side,
In your small yard off the suburban road.
He stretches a little in young manhood's pride
Broadening his shoulders for the longed-for load,
The wife that he has won, a home his own;
His growing powers hidden as spring, unknown,
But surging in him toward their certain birth,
Explosive as dandelions in the earth.

She leans upon his arm, as if to hide
A strength perhaps too forward for a bride,
Feminine in her bustle and long skirt;
She looks demure, with just a touch of flirt
In archly tilted head and squinting smile
At the photographer, she watches while
Pretending to be a girl, although so strong,
Playing the role of wife ("Here I belong!"),
Anticipating mother, with man for child,
Amused at all her roles, unreconciled.

And I who gaze at you and recognize
The budding gestures that were soon to be
My cradle and my home, my trees, my skies,
I am your child, staring at you with eyes
Of love and grief for parents who have died;
But also with omniscience born of time,
Seeing your unlined faces, dreams untried,
Your tentativeness and your brave attack,
I am no longer daughter gazing back;
I am your mother, watching far ahead,
Seeing events so clearly now they're gone
And both of you are dead, and I alone,
And in my own life now already past
That garden in the grass where you two stand.
I long to comfort you for all you two
In time to come must meet and suffer through,
To answer with a hindsight-given truth
The questions in those wondering eyes of youth.
I long to tell you, starting on your quest,
"You'll do it all, you know, you'll meet the test."

Mother compassionate and child bereft
I am; the past and present, wisdom and innocence,
Fused by one flicker of a camera lens
Some stranger snapped in laughter as he left
More than a half a century ago—
My children, my parents.

ANNE MORROW LINDBERGH

'TO ENDURE THE ORDEAL OF LOVING'

Author of Friendly Persuasion, *Jessamyn West writes about the difference between being in love and loving in* Love Is Not What You Think:

"Falling in love," "being in love," as differentiated from loving, are intoxicating states for many reasons. Whatever the age, whatever the reasons for the fall, one feels when in love that nothing else matters. One is turned wholly toward the loved one. There are no longer any trivialities in life. Those that do not relate to the loved one do not exist; those that do are not trivial. It has all the concentrating power of war or tennis—which is to say of death and competition—but a concentration that, unlike them, is suffused with a desire to please, not to defeat or harm. In love, a woman feels Biblical; she has put first things first. The woman in love has the conviction, for which we all long, that her life is unified, that it has direction and meaning, that its direction is toward, and its meaning suffused with, the truth, that in love she transcends time and makes herself one with forces which are eternal. Her convictions are not without foundation.

How useless it is to say to the girl or woman in love, "What do you see in that man?" It is not

against the man you must argue, if you are fool-
ish enough to argue, but against the woman herself and the feelings that flood and transform her.
She is the one who must be refuted, and this is a
man-sized job, capable of accomplishment sometimes only by the man with whom she has fallen
in love.

The woman may not yet love, in any of the
true meanings of that word, the man or boy who
has elicited these feelings; but she does love the
person she has become: a woman purified by
love's focusing, a woman who longs to serve and
to sacrifice, a woman whose desire it is to be
wholly used. All of her intuition tells her that
when she feels thus, she is most herself and most
woman, a person from whom she can never, except tragically, alienate herself.

Paradoxical as it may seem, it is the loving, not
the loved, woman who feels lovable. Being loved
may very well be nothing but the sign of some
man's blind stupidity. Loving is the result of
your own astuteness; it is a state that imagines
reciprocity and hence lovableness. This does not
mean that woman feels worthy, only that her
great love lifts her to a height where the man
may, out of his goodness, and by bending low,
reach her. In love, asking to have much asked of
her, the woman feels herself to be nearest that

best self whom she never, in the longest, blackest life, wholly forgets. For this reason, the woman who has loved, whether in conformity to or in transgression of the world's rules, has climbed one rung higher on heaven's ladder than the woman who has never known this desire to serve, to sacrifice, to lose herself in another. . . .

"Falling in love," unlike loving, does not know disappointment or defeat. "Being in love" is not love lived out. Nothing is yet put to trial. Women "in love" are summer soldiers. Where will they be when the snow flies? At this stage they are civilians ready to die for their country every time the band plays "The Stars and Stripes Forever." Every man is a hero far from the bayonet; every woman is a heroine of love until she starts practicing that arduous craft—particularly with the man with whom she has fallen in love. . . .

But a desire to be "in love" is the first step in that sensational and downward path where finally to feel anything and by any means is a boon.

"Falling in love," except as a focusing and a revelation, has about the same relation to love as the idea for a story has to the ordeal of its writing. Without the afflatus of the original vision, the story might never be attempted. The attempt to body it forth may cause the writer agony, tears of defeat, and disappointment. Still, he must make up his mind whether he wants to be a writer or a dreamer, and the same holds true with love. "Falling in love" is not an end in itself; it is the vision that enables us to embark upon and, if it is strong enough and we are strong enough, to endure the ordeal of loving.

'WORTHY OF LOVE AND HONOR'

Author Ruth Stout takes a close look at marriage vows in this selection from her book It's A Woman's World:

Recently I attended a wedding. The bride was glowing. I don't know about a groom, but I believe that every young bride, if she's marrying for love, feels that the thrill and romance will last forever, despite the less-than-inspiring marriages she has probably observed. The word "obey" has been deleted from the ceremony, which seems to me a step forward, but "love" and "honor" remained. I remember when women began to make a stand against promising to obey a husband; good for them, I thought, but I didn't understand (and I still don't) why they were willing to promise to love and honor a man for the rest of their lives. You can at least keep a vow

to obey, if you want to, but no amount of determination and will power and good faith will help you to continue to love and honor anyone; that takes other ingredients which may be out of your power, or the other person's, to supply. I should think it would be more reasonable to have each one promise to try to be worthy of love and honor; that would at least be something one could work for.

'THE HIGHEST ROMANCE'

Novelist Pearl Buck, many of whose books are set in the mysterious Orient, dispels some of the mysteries about marriage in her book, To My Daughters with Love. *In this selection she answers the question," what shall I tell my daughter when she marries?"*

I will speak to her of something more important than love. I will speak to her of herself.

I will say to her something like this:

"The question is not whether you ever stop loving him or he ever stops loving you. The question is, do you know who you are? Well, I will tell you. You are a woman. In many ways you are a fortunate woman. You have beauty, you have intelligence. But these are perquisites and not necessities. They are gifts for which you should be thankful, and which you should use to the utmost. But if you had not these gifts, you would still be a woman and you would still have the necessity to know what it means to be a woman.

"You ask what this means? It means that you are a creation entirely different from man. True, nature does not discriminate between male and female in the distribution of her gifts. A daughter may inherit the brains and not the son. She may have much while he may have little. Yet the fact that you have intelligence does not mean the same as the man material. It is as though clear spring water were poured into a rose-red glass bowl and appeared rose red. If the same spring water were poured into a blue-glass bowl it would appear blue. Essentially it is the same but the container changes the hue. You will have the same impulses that Peter has, certainly the same need for love, but it will be expressed differently. . . .

"Your love permeates your whole being. You are fortunate in the many ways you have of expressing love. To arrange his house, to plan his meals, to care for his comfort, to serve him— yes, I insist upon the word, for such service is sacred to love, even in the simplest and most menial ways. Menial? Nothing is menial where there is love.

"I tell you frankly that you must teach him the many ways of expressing love. . . . Above all, do not blame him for ignorance about you. You see why you must not be ignorant about yourself. If you do not understand yourself as a woman, how can you teach him?

"And let him teach you about himself. Do not pretend to know everything. You are ignorant about him because you are not a man, just as he is ignorant about you because he is not a woman. Teach one another and rejoice in being so taught. The more each knows of the other, the happier both will be. And you will never know everything, either of you, for in this mutual teaching— from the smallest detail, as for example how he likes his coffee, to the deepest and most profound matter of private love—you will discover that you are both growing and developing and reaching new levels of emotion and intelligence. There is nothing so fertilizing to the growth of the individual man and woman as the love between them, a growing, living love, which is to say, true, love. He will never stop loving you if he finds something always new in you, and through you in himself. Nor will you ever stop loving him. Love dies only when growth stops.

"What was it that a wise old Chinese said five hundred years before our Christian era? A disciple asked him whether a certain way was the right way, and Laotze replied: 'It is a way, but not the eternal way.'

"You may test the truth of your love by your own growth as a woman and his as a man. . . .

"Yet do not worry yourself or even inquire of yourself as to whether you are growing. You will know that you are growing, for love will keep you informed. You will be happy—yes, even though there may be occasional disagreement. I will not use the word quarrel, for only children quarrel, without regard to facts or truth. Never descend to such trifling behavior with him. It is not important to know *who* is right. It is only important to know *what* is right. And you will discover that truth together and only together. A one-sided conclusion, declared by one against the other, will be only a half truth and worth nothing. The one who insists and prevails by insistence takes the first step toward the death of love. Do not compete with him, for competition is impossible between you. Neither can lose and neither wins. I deny the battle of the sexes. If we do battle, then the battle is already lost for both. Victory is only to be achieved in unity—victory over life and, yes, over death.

"Accept your womanhood, my daughter, and rejoice in it. It is your glory that you are a woman, for this is why he loves you, he whom you love . . . . Through your love, teach him what it means to be a man, a noble man, a strong man. Believe in him, for only through your belief can he believe in himself. In our secret hearts, man and woman, we long above all else to know that the other, the one we love, knows what we are and believes in what we can be. Is this not romance? Yes, and the highest romance, investing the smallest detail of life with the color of joy."

'TO PASS FROM LOVE TO FRIENDSHIP'

French author and man of letters Andre Maurois compares the oneness in marriage to a "richly embroidered cloth lined with another":
The whole art of marriage lies in the ability to pass from love to friendship without sacrificing love. It is not utterly impossible. The white heat of passion sometimes burns to the very end, but where husband and wife are really one, "that magnificent silk, so richly embroidered, is lined with another, simpler, but of so rare and fine a texture that one is tempted to prefer it to what covers it." The dominant note, then, is one of

confidence, whose perfection is matched by the degree of mutual understanding which goes with it and an affection so watchful that it foresees the reactions of the beloved.

THE JOYS IN LOVING

In their book To Marry With Love, *Virginia and Louis Baldwin suggest that joy in marriage is based on a mutual and constant effort to share and understand:*

Nothing can guarantee you happiness. It isn't something served on a platter, silver or otherwise, by your partner or anyone else. The more you demand from your marriage, the less you are likely to get. But if you'll accept the proposition that happiness depends on your love for your partner more than on your partner's love for you, you will change the odds radically in your favor.

Marriage is not a state of perpetual ecstasy. It's a lot better if you recognize this before you get married rather than learn it the hard way afterward. A good marriage—which means a continually improving marriage—is a spiritual experience, not a kind of glandular fever. Its joys are in the constant, loving effort to understand

and help each other. Its happiness is in learning to share, in the lifelong transformation of "alone" into "together." Such a marriage takes work, like any other worthwhile human adventure. But the work is a joy if it is infused with spiritual love, if you desire your partner's happiness as much as you desire your own. Only in seeking your partner's happiness will you ever find your own.

'THEY HAVE SURVIVED EVERYTHING'

In his essay 'Love and Marriage,' *author Ernest Havemann describes the golden years of marriage, the marriage that has endured through "everything that life could throw" at it:*

You can see them alongside the shuffleboard courts in Florida or on the porches of the old folks' homes up north: an old man with snow-white hair, a little hard of hearing, reading the newspaper through a magnifying glass; an old woman in a shapeless dress, her knuckles gnarled by arthritis, wearing sandals to ease her aching arches. They are holding hands, and in a little while they will totter off to take a nap, and then she will cook supper, not a very good supper, and they will watch television, until it is time for

bed. They may even have a good, soul-stirring argument, just to prove that they still really care. And through the night they will snore unabashedly, each resting content because the other is there. They are in love, they have always been in love, although sometimes they would have denied it. And because they have been in love they have survived everything that life could throw at them, even their own failures.

'OURS IS A TRUE PROFESSION'

Poet and mother of two daughters, Phyllis Mc-Ginley here lauds the housewife, who, despite lack of recognition from the Nobel Prize Committee, does an award-winning job:

God must love housewives as He does the poor. He makes so many of us. . . . Because we are so many, we are sometimes downgraded in our own eyes. We form no unions, belong to no professional organizations. We do not federate, lobby in the Senate, go on strike, scream for shorter working days, or establish corporations. Our hours are peculiar, our wages irregular. Few honors come to us in the shape of scrolls or Doctorates or Chairmanships of Foundations named with our names. If we have any public status apart from that which our husbands' abilities bring us, it is limited and local. Nobody has so far received a Pulitzer Prize for contriving a poetic boiled custard, in spite of the fact (which I know from experience) that it is a feat less easy to perform than writing a ballade. The Nobel Committee has yet to award any laurels to a woman simply for making her home a place of such peace and delight that her family might rightfully rise up and call her blessed—if such an odd notion ever occurred to them.

Nevertheless, ours is a true profession, ancient, honorable, and unique. . . . When some early and talented woman patted her barley cake into a pleasanter shape than her neighbor's, or poured honey on it for a change from drippings, she was advancing her profession and, with it, civilization. When she complained that the floors were cold and persuaded her husband to let her use that extra bearskin for protection against drafts from the doorway, she was progressing another step along the route. It is true that most useful novelties, from the wheel to paper napkins and Scotch tape, have been conceived of first by men. But I suspect it was a housewife who fostered the notions to begin with.

"Really dear, the children oughtn't be sleeping on the floor," I can hear her saying to her man some winter night. "Why don't you invent a Bed?"

Or even, "Day in, day out, nothing but raw meat. I declare, I'm tired of it. Father, you're a clever fellow. How about discovering Fire?"

It encourages me to remember that I belong to such an old and continuous company. . . . On us rests the burden (and the glory) of seeing to it that the pot boils, the table is set, the sheets get changed, the babies remain healthy, a light shines in the window after dark, and there is re-freshment for body and spirit waiting at the day's end. . . .

We crave light and warmth in this century. Only the mother, the wife, can supply it for the home. To be a housewife is not easy. Ours is a difficult, a wrenching, sometimes an ungrateful job if it is looked on only as a job. Regarded as a profession, it is the noblest as it is the most ancient of the catalog. Let none persuade us dif-ferently or the world is lost indeed.

Mother and Child

A PRECIOUS MOMENT

In The Story of the Trapp Family Singers, *now immortalized by the movie* The Sound of Music, *Maria Augusta Trapp describes with moving warmth the birth of her child. Here she thanks God for the baby's good health:*

During the first weeks of the nine months, we had been rather choosy. It should be a boy—blond-haired, blue-eyed, tall and thin. Georg wanted him to look like his mother, whereas I definitely wanted him to be the image of my hero. The closer time came the less fussy we were. If he is only healthy with straight arms and legs, even the color of eyes and hair wouldn't matter any more. And right now it was just the same whether it was a boy or a girl. All the strength of the whole being was concentrated on the one thing necessary:

"Oh God, help, help that this Thy child be born healthy in body and soul."

When a piercing little shriek cut through the solemn silence, I heard the children downstairs jump from their seats and jubilantly break into the hymn of thanksgiving by the old master

Bach: "Now Thank We All Our God," while Georg was leaning over me, kissing me on the forehead. In these precious moments the human being feels lifted up into the heights of God, partaking of His power, a co-worker of God, the Father, Creator of heaven and earth.

'I LOVE APRONS'

In her book Marlene Dietrich's ABC, *Miss Dietrich praises aprons and what they symbolize:*
I love aprons. The large white ones with the broad bands and large square pockets. Before "The Lighthouse for the Blind" had them for sale, I used to buy nurses' aprons, the old-fashioned kind with all-around gathers. Pockets in a clinging apron don't mean much.

A woman in an apron invites hugging. The apron of a woman flung over a kitchen chair is a wonderful still life. And the pockets of that apron, harboring sticky unwrapped candies, crumpled bits of paper, newspaper ads hastily torn out, pennies and nickles and a ribbon stuck to a band-aid, a baby's sock and a bottle cap should be food for poets who are so easily tempted to linger on the treasures in a little boy's pants pocket.

JUST YESTERDAY

It's just a step from yesterday,
from baby's toes to stocking's run;
the tantrum and the nursery rhyme
practice their difficult duets.
The faded lace-trimmed valentine
signs treaties on the telephone
to end a war that's just begun.

Which is the woman, which the child?
The joyous laugh that opens doors,
steals sugared moments from the shelf?
Or the dreamer mixing metaphors
with tears to make a book of self
to read aloud in winter's rooms
when summer's sounds
have ceased to bloom?

Curious, the way the infant crawls
from innocent to dissembling:
yesterday reached for a doll;
today stands tall and trembling
at tomorrow's terrible reach
as if hoping she might keep
her child heart from a greedy world.

                              KATIE LOUCHHEIM

'WHAT MORE IMPORTANT JOB
IS THERE?'

Author Edith Hunter in her book Woman: The
Teacher of Values *describes the importance of
women in the home. Here she lauds the educated
woman in her important role of transmitting
values to children:*

Both men and women live through the same
cycle of birth, growth, maturity and death, but
nature has, to some extent, circumscribed the
context in which most women mature. Women
always have, and I imagine always will, bear the
children of the world. No culture has as yet
worked out a variation on this.

It is a fact, therefore, that for a large portion of
our maturity, perhaps twenty-five years, we will
be living intimately with the children we bear. If
we undertake the major care of the children before they start the first grade, and my premise is
that the mothers should, we will have a great
deal to do with the kind of persons they become
and they will have a great deal to do with the
kind of persons we become.

Sometimes, when we read of the plight of
modern women, it sounds as if the primary
problem facing us is that so many educated
women are "ending up" in the home, instead of

being out in the world doing something significant.

Educated women in the home? What an odd thing to deplore! What better place to have us "end up," although it might be more accurate to say "live," since children do usually grow up before we end up. What more important job is there than sharing the values we are learning to cherish with the next generation of adults? What more strategic place could there be for educated women?

'THE MODERN MOTHER'

Anthropologist Margaret Mead, whose studies of different cultures have spanned more than 40 years and brought her national acclaim, concentrates her knowledge of familial relationships in her book, Family. *In this selection she describes a child's need for a mother's "unconditional love":*

Modern women are freed from the terrors of the unknown, the dangers of giving birth in the dark and the cold, the anxieties of meeting an infant's need for food—the worst difficulties that haunted the imagination of primitive women. But civilization confronts us with difficulties of our

own making and sets new conditions for mother-hood.

Yet the modern mother still is asked to love her child unconditionally, and the child now, as in the past, is dependent on her unconditional love. The child who has experienced safety, warmth, and comfort in its mother's arms carries with it a sense of personal worth and of trust in human relationships that makes tolerable the tasks and difficulties that must be faced later in life. The child whose mother has succeeded in giving it a sense of being valued as a unique individual, entirely for itself, without regard for the accidents of beauty or brains or special talent, is prepared as a person to meet the challenges of living. We do not know—man has never known—how else to give a human being a sense of selfhood and identity, a sense of the worth of the world, and an abiding trust in human relationships. Without these, growing up is very hard, and sometimes may be impossible.

As we find ways of supplementing the mother's single, often frail and insufficient body, and of making more flexible the bonds between mother and child, we are also making the discovery that there is no substitute for the mothering relationship. For this reason, in spite of all the changes that have been introduced by modern inventions, the model for motherhood remains what it has been—the relationship between the mother's body and the body of her child. . . . And the central image of the mother's physical care and love for a small human being who has been and continues to be wholly dependent on her for its life and health carries with it the proviso of the mother's absolute acceptance of her child. Faced by a child who cannot thrive on her love, a mother is helpless. But the love and care a child evokes in its mother does not depend on whether it is beautiful or homely, plump or thin, fretful or content; as long as it lives—and, hopefully, thrives—it is hers to care for. It is this absolute, unconditional acceptance that every child needs. Lacking it, a human being never ceases to seek it. . . .

Every act of motherhood contains a dual intent, as the mother holds the child close and prepares it to move away from her, as she supports the child and stands it firmly on its own feet, and as she guards it against danger and sends it out across the yard, down by the stream, and across the traffic-crowded highway. Unless a mother can do both—gather her child close and turn her child out toward the world—she will fail in her purpose. . . .

For the child must go forth from the warmth

and safety of its mother's care—first to take a few steps across the room, then to join playmates, and later to go to school, to work, to experience courtship and marriage, and to establish a new home. A boy must learn how different he is from his mother; he must learn that his life is turned outward to the world. A girl must learn, as she walks beside her mother, that she is both like her mother and a person in her own right. It is one of the basic complications of a mother's life that she must teach one thing to her sons and other things to her daughters.

Famous for Their Love

Queen Victoria, although a strong, self-assertive woman, privately deferred to her quiet husband, in whom she put her trust, affection, and devotion. In his biography Albert Prince Consort, *author Hector Bolitho captures the essence of their unique marriage. Here, the gentle Albert wins the devotion of his sometimes wilful queen through kindness and example:*

The Queen watched Prince Albert treading his cautious way and she constantly thanked God for the blessing of her marriage. She wrote in her journal, "I *know what REAL happiness* is." Only italics and capitals could celebrate her gratitude. Soon after the Prince of Wales was born, Lady Lyttleton was brought into the Court to take care of him, and she remained until he was seven years old. She wrote of the 'vein of iron' running through the Queen's 'extraordinary character.' But this hardness lessened, as her fears lessened; as she allowed her affection to govern her actions, and as she learned to accept the fact that Prince Albert's intellect was greater than her own. Even Stockmar [friend and mentor of Prince Albert] came to acknowledge the achievements of his pupil. During his visit to England, early in 1842, Lord Aberdeen told him how gratified ministers were "to perceive that the Queen leant upon the Prince's judgment, and showed an obvious desire that he should share her duties." . . .

The Queen's early, nervous haughtiness of manner was fading: her faith in [Prime Minister Robert] Peel was related to the private security that she now enjoyed with her husband. Her fear, before their marriage, that Prince Albert might endeavor to 'oppose' her, had changed into a fear that he might not be exalted enough. In February 1845 she wished him to be created 'King Consort,' and she wrote in her journal, "He ought to be, and is above me in everything really, and therefore I wish that he should be equal in rank to me." . . .

During the change of government [with Lord John Russell as Prime Minister], the Queen had written to her uncle, "Albert's use to me, and I may say to the *Country*, by firmness and sagacity, is beyond all belief in these moments of trial." She wrote also, "Everywhere my dearest Angel receives the respect and honours I receive." But this was not true. He was still a

minor prince to the haughty English aristocracy.
. . . Many of the aristocracy clung to Lord Ches-
terfield's view that "a man of fashion, who is seen
piping or fiddling at a concert, degrades his own
dignity," and they were chagrined because of
Prince Albert's liking for scientists, artists, and
musicians. . . .

In spite of the discords in the world beyond
the Castle walls, the Queen and the Prince
created their own happiness. . . .

*In 1851, the Great Exhibition, for which the
Crystal Palace was built, opened. Although pub-
lic opinion and the press were at first against the
Exhibition, Prince Albert's brain child, they
changed their minds when it was completed.
Queen Victoria was gratified:*

The first day of May 1851 was the proudest in
the Prince's public life. The Queen walked into
the Crystal Palace, beside him, and with their
two eldest children. She wore a dress of pink
watered silk, brocaded with silver and diamonds.
She went to her Chair of State, but it was Prince
Albert's victory she was celebrating; his victory
over an apathetic people who disliked foreign-
ers; over an aristocracy and a hierarchy that re-
sented his moral seriousness, and over the
Queen's own early wilfulness and pride. They
walked among the exhibits, followed by the first

52

of the six million subjects who were to see the wonders before the summer ended. 'God bless my dearest Albert. God bless my dearest country,' the Queen wrote when the day was over. Then, 'All is owing to Albert—All to him.'

ADAM AND EVE

Here humorist Mark Twain tells a tongue-in-cheek story about the first marriage, that of Adam and Eve. His conclusion, however, is a touching tribute to "the new creature," Eve:

MONDAY—This new creature with the long hair is a good deal in the way. It is always hanging around and following me about. I don't like this; I am not used to company. I wish it would stay with the other animals. . . . Think we shall have rain. . . . *We?* Where did I get that word? I remember now—the new creature uses it. . . .

WEDNESDAY—Built me a shelter against the rain, but could not have it to myself in peace. The new creature intruded. When I tried to put it out it shed water out of the holes it looks with and wiped it away with the back of its paws, and made a noise such as some of the other animals make when they are in distress. I wish it would not talk. It is always talking. . . .

MONDAY—The new creature says its name is Eve. That is all right. I have no objections. Says it is to call it by when I want it to come. I said it was superfluous, then. . . .

SATURDAY—I escaped last Tuesday night and traveled two days, and built me another shelter in a secluded place, and obliterated my tracks as well as I could, but she hunted me out . . . and came making that pitiful noise again, and shedding that water out of the place she looks with. I was obliged to return with her, but will presently emigrate again when occasion offers. . . .

TUESDAY—She has taken up with a snake now. . . . I am glad because the snake talks and this enables me to get a rest.

FRIDAY—She says the snake advises her to try fruit of that tree and says the result will be a great and fine and noble education. I told her there would be another result too—it would introduce death into the world. . . . I advised her to keep away from the tree. She said she wouldn't. I foresee trouble. Will emigrate. . . .

WEDNESDAY—I escaped last night and rode a horse all night as fast as he could go. . . . About an hour after sun-up, I was riding through a flowery plain where thousands of animals were grazing. . . . All of a sudden they broke into a tempest of frightful noises and in one moment the plain was a frantic commotion and every beast was destroying its neighbor. I knew what it meant—Eve had eaten that fruit and death was coming into the world. . . . I found this place, outside the Park and was fairly comfortable for a few days but she has found me out. . . . In fact, I was not sorry she came, for there are but meager pickings here and she brought some of those apples. I was obliged to eat them, I was so hungry. It was against my principles but I find that principles have no real force except when one is well fed. . . . I find she is a good deal of a companion. I see I should be lonesome and depressed without her now that I have lost my property. . . . She says it is ordered that we work for our living hereafter. She will be useful. I will superintend.

TEN YEARS LATER— . . . After all these years, I see that I was mistaken about Eve in the beginning; it is better to live outside the Garden with her than inside it without her. At first I thought she talked too much; but now I should be sorry to have that voice fall silent and pass out of my life. Blessed be the fruit that brought us near together and taught me to know the goodness of her heart and the sweetness of her spirit! . . .

AT EVE'S GRAVE—Wheresoever she was, *there* was Eden.

A LIFE INFINITELY GRANDER

The fervent and touching love shared by President Woodrow Wilson and his wife, Ellen, is revealed in the letters they exchanged during their courtship and marriage. Their daughter, Eleanor Wilson McAdoo, has published some of their 1,400 letters in The Priceless Gift. *Ellen Wilson emerges as a gentle and loving wife who "avoided the limelight in order to remain a constant, private source of love and encouragement for her husband." Ellen writes:*

I wish there had been sacrifices for me to make that I might prove by such means how I prize your love. But there is no sacrifice possible because you give me with yourself everything;— you satisfy every possible need of my nature; my heart and mind are both filled. You have given me someone—the right one—to love and trust and believe in perfectly, to look up to and honour entirely. And then, darling, how you satisfy my pride and ambition. You don't know how I glory in your splendid gifts, your noble character, that rare charm of manner and "presence." And as for ambitions, mine are destined to be much more fully satisfied than ever yours will be, because, you see, I am so fully satisfied with what you do, while you will never be. By the same rule how much greater is my delight in your triumphs than it could ever have been in any little success of my own. Ah, it is a great thing to be the wife of such a man! how much greater to be one with him and follow him in his noble progress than to move on in one's own little narrow orbit! The universe itself seems somehow to grow greater, and life to be infinitely grander and more precious and better worth living. . . .

Mrs. McAdoo describes an incident that reveals how much the Wilsons cherished their closeness: On March the third, 1913, [the eve of the inauguration] Woodrow and Ellen came out of the house on Cleveland Lane, looked at the newsmen, the Secret Service and a large, loaned automobile, and suddenly rebelled. They would walk, alone, to the station, Woodrow announced, and no one dared to protest.

The President-elect and his wife made a detour. Library Place was not on the way to the station, but they wanted to pass by the house which they had struggled and worked and saved to build. It was not a sad pilgrimage. They had worked for this day too. But they knew what lay ahead and they needed one last glimpse of the place where, for seven happy years, they had lived with peace. . . .

[As the President's wife] the number and variety of her duties had appalled her at first but not for long. She planned each day in advance, hour by hour, except Sundays, which were devoted exclusively, after church, to quiet afternoons and evenings with her family. But her schedule was never so rigidly adhered to that she could not interrupt it instantly when Woodrow needed her for counsel and encouragement, and she included nothing which she did not consider directly, or indirectly, helpful to him.

'LOVE MAKES A LEVEL'

Against the objections of both her father and the Browning family, Elizabeth Barrett married Robert Browning. She was six years his senior and an invalid. Elizabeth Barrett Browning immortalized her love for her husband in her sonnet, "How Do I Love Thee?" Here, in a letter to her sisters, she speaks eloquently of the regard and devotion she and her husband shared:

But those who question most, will do him justice fullest—and we must wait a little with resignation [for Father's approval]. In the meanwhile, what he is, and what he is to *me*, I would fain teach you. —Have faith in me to believe it. He

58

puts out all his great faculties to give me pleasure and comfort . . . charms me into thinking of *him* when he sees my thoughts wandering . . . forces me to smile in spite of all of them—if you had seen that day at Orleans. . . .

He loves me more and more. Today we have been together a fortnight, and he said to me with a deep, serious tenderness . . . "I kissed your feet, my Ba, before I married you—but now I would kiss the ground under your feet, I love with a so much greater love." And this is true, I see and feel. I feel to have it in my hands. It is strange that anyone so brilliant should love *me*, —but true and strange it is . . . and it is impossible for me to doubt it any more. Perfectly happy therefore we should be. . . .

I must not forget to tell you what Mrs. Jameson said the other day to me. . . . "Well, it is the most charming thing to see you and Mr. Browning together. If two persons were to be chosen from the ends of the earth for perfect union and fitness, there could not be a greater congruity than between you two—" which I tell you, because I think it will please you to hear what is an honest impression of hers, though far too great a compliment to me. . . . And for the rest, if he is brilliant and I am dull, (socially speaking) *Love makes a level*, which is my comfort. . . .

Mrs. Browning's most famous sonnet appeared in Sonnets From the Portuguese, *a collection of love poems dedicated to Robert Browning and written secretly during their courtship:*

How do I love thee? Let me count the ways.
I love thee to the depth and breadth and height
My soul can reach, when feeling out of sight
For the ends of Being and Ideal Grace.
I love thee to the level of every day's
Most quiet need, by sun and candlelight.
I love thee freely, as men strive for Right;
I love thee purely, as they turn from Praise;
I love thee with the passion put to use
In my old griefs, and with my childhood's faith;
I love thee with a love I seemed to lose
With my lost saints,—I love thee with the breath,
Smiles, tears, of all my life!—and, if God choose,
I shall but love thee better after death.

Set in Weiss Roman, designed by Emil Rudolf Weiss
for the Bauer Typographic Foundry. Typography by
Joseph Thuringer and set at the Rochester Typographic
Service. Printed on Hallmark Eggshell Book Paper.
Designed by William M. Gilmore